CHINESE-JAPANESE
COOK-BOOK

CHINESE - JAPANESE
COOK BOOK

BY
SARA BOSSE
AND
ONOTO WATANNA

APPLEWOOD BOOKS
Bedford, Massachusetts

This cookbook has been reprinted in cooperation with
the Culinary Trust, which is the philanthropic arm of the
International Association of Culinary Professionals (IACP).
The Trust celebrates the culinary past and future by funding
educational and charitable programs related to the culinary
industry (including scholarships for students and career professionals; library research and travel grants for food writers),
cookbook preservation and restoration; and hunger alleviation.
Tax-deductible gifts to the Culinary Trust should be sent to:

The Culinary Trust
304 West Liberty Street, Suite 201
Louisville, KY 40202
Web site: www.theculinarytrust.com
Phone: (502) 581-9786 x264

Thank you for purchasing an Applewood book. Applewood
reprints America's lively classics—books from the past that are
still of interest to modern readers. For a free copy of our current
catalog, write to:

Applewood Books
P.O. Box 365
Bedford, MA 01730

ISBN 1-55709-371-7

10 9 8 7 6 5 4 3 2 1

An Introduction to the
CHINESE-JAPANESE COOK BOOK

Jacqueline M. Newman

Fascination comes with exploration; examining nuances in this fantastic out-of-print 1914 cookbook is no exception. It is a gem because it looks at what was common in those days. Chinoiserie was adored earlier by Thomas Jefferson who ordered and used Chinese tea service and planted Chinese vegetables. It was adored by Benjamin Franklin who wrote to Jefferson about things Chinese. It was adored in times when Chinese food was devoured literally and by reading about it and other Asian foods.

This book has many interesting recipes, particularly among the Chinese set. For example, few early or later Chinese cookbooks use water chestnut flour. Rare is the one with recipes for bird's nests. Hardly ever was there one with chicken and pork in a single chop suey recipe. Exceptional is the "pickle" recipe called Chinese Pickled Yellow Turnips. I recall eating it at Chinese homes in the late 1930s and early 1940s including at my mom's Chinese friend's home. The recipe for *Lai Yut*, also called Moon Tarts, is also a gem. This rarity is now called Moon Cakes. In years past, the Chinese hunted geese. This recipe uses their clarified fat and incorporates lychee paste. Instructions to make it are included.

The copy on my desk has reddish-brown fabric-covered boards. Pasted on the front is a picture of a Japanese lady in kimono and obi. Its size is 16.6 x 10 cm, the front board corners square, the gilt lettering on front and spine now worn. Inside is information and recipes, two pages of advertising with one page showing three other books by Rand McNally, the reverse side with an ad for their *House of Good Juveniles*.

Ravenna Rare Books, a dealer in Seattle, Washington once listed a slightly different copy. Theirs was but 16.6 by 8.4 centimeters, its cover brown, boards with rounded corners, end-papers depicting a pattern of ½ x 5/16 inch squares and a man outside the door of an inn ringing a dinner gong with spoon and pan. The initials H.M. by J.W. appear on their copy, the HM and JW stand for *Hotel Monthly* and John Willy, the publisher. Theirs has one advertising leaf at the end for *The Hotel Monthly Handbook* they published. It is not uncommon to find several different editions in early Chinese and Japanese cookbooks; were there others?

A 1994 article, "Decoding Onoto Watanna" by Yuko Matsukawa in *Tricksterism in Turn-of-the-century American Literature* (Elizabeth Ammons and Annette White-Parks, editors; London: University Press of New England, pp. 104–25) indicates this book is full of tricks. One such, the Eaton sisters given names, Edith (1865–1914) and Winnifred (1875–1954). They are Anglo-Saxon, of Anglo-Chinese descent, and among the earliest of Asian–American writers. Edith assumes the pen name Sui Sin Far, and writes short stories about Chinese–

American communities on America's west coast. Winnifred takes the pseudonym Onoto Watanna, writing popular romances with Japanese and American characters. For her first name, she uses the 'pen' name of a Japanese fountain pen called the Onoto. It was made by the Thomas de la Rue Company and uses it with permission. Is it a trick for her fictitious Japanese identity? Why that name tom-foolery, and why the Japanese lady wearing a beautiful blue kimono on the cover of my copy. She is kneeling and using her right hand to stir a bowl of hot rice or hot soup? It is sending forth lots of steam advising the book is full of hot air?

The Chinese and Japanese sections are dissimilar. The Chinese one has sixty pages and sixty-two recipes in eleven recipe sections, and "Rules for Cooking." The Japanese one has forty pages with forty-seven recipes, and a list titled "Chinese and Japanese Groceries." The recipes indicate more expertise in Chinese–American cookery. If the preface is to be believed, the recipes were handed down "from a worthy descendant of a long line of noted Chinese cooks" and attributed to "high Mandarins from Shanghai." As most are distinctly Cantonese matching the immigrant population of their times, is this another trick?

Mama Eaton is Chinese and adopted at age three by English missionaries. Their father is British and all live in the United States. The writers say the recipes can be cooked and served in any American home. We see them as simple Chinese–American ones using ordinary ingredients. Many are for chop suey and chow mein using lots of celery, bean sprouts, and gravy. They imitate the cooking of the few Chinese immigrants in the United States, most from Guangzhou. The Japanese meat and fish recipes are also simple even though several use rabbit, pheasant, venison pigeon, even whale; the vegetable dishes more Chinese than Japanese. Desserts straddle both cuisines.

This 1914 dual Asian cookery-culture English-language cookbook is the first of a multi-cultural Asian genre. There are three Chinese one that precede it (Blasdale, 1899; Gilbreth, 1910, and Nolton,1911) and another published the same year (Garner, 1914). It is the second English-language cookbook located with Japanese recipes published in the United States, the first a Japanese reprint done in 1901 in Oakland, California.

Did the authors like Chinese and Japanese food or is the book a trick to cover their other concerns? They say, "When it is known how simple and clean are the ingredients used to make up these Oriental dishes, the Westerner will cease to feel that natural repugnance which assails one when about to taste a strange dish of a new and strange land." Did they like Asian foods? There is no indication their mom actually cooked Chinese or Japanese food for them, her husband, or her fourteen other children. Did she know the foods of her heritage? Did she share it with these daughters, or is this book a search for their roots or another trick?

Winnifred's first pen name means 'to cross' and may sound Japanese, but it is not. Is this crossing another trick? The Japanese recipes seem more Chinese than Japanese, the former attributed to someone from Shanghai. How would a chef from there know about chop suey and chow mein? The authors recommend going to restaurants to taste various Chinese and Japanese dishes. In 1914 and years before, most Chinese restaurants in the United States served Cantonese food; rare was the chef from Shanghai. Even more rare was a Japanese restaurant chef, so is that another trick?

Yoko Matsukawa, who wrote the cited article, believes the recipes are from local restaurants catering to Chinese-Americans. She believes the authors are defining their own ethnicity and that by tricking they blur boundaries of Chinese and Japanese food. When the book was written, people were fascinated with Asia and Asians, but knew little about these countries or their cuisines. The authors were more knowledgeable because their father made many trips to the countries they wrote about. Their others books were fiction; is this one more story than reality? Is that why the recipe for Boiled and Deviled Cucumbers slices them, serves them with olive oil, vinegar, and cayenne powder and beats in yolks of hard-boiled eggs? Are these yokes another joke?

In spite of or because of the many tricks, there is a lot to learn from this dual-culture cookery volume. For example, no other Chinese cookbook has a recipe for Extra White Chop Suey, none has one for Pineapple Fish using two pounds of fish cooked for thirty-five minutes. None has a Meat Chow Mein recipe or any other using half pound of dried mushrooms. None advises never to wash saucepans with soap but to use washing soda or sand. None says "meat should not be washed, but should be rinsed in cold or lukewarm water and, if necessary, singed over a hot flame and scraped with a hot knife." Did these sisters live near a family that kept kosher and they learned this poultry-cleaning advise from them? No other Chinese cookbook advises that vegetables and fruit be washed in cold water and if necessary, done fifty times.

Learn from its cooking rules, recipes, writing style, and ingredient amounts. They deserve careful perusal. They may also be the ultimate tricks. Before 1920, Chinese cookbooks published in the United States had similar simple recipes. Twenty years later more authentic recipes appear. So, while careful reading does bring laughs, more importantly it teaches lessons and love of the authors efforts to educate Westerners about Asian heritages, as known at that time.

Jacqueline M. Newman is a Professor Emeritus at Queens College and Editor of Flavor and Fortune, *a Chinese food magazine.*

CONTENTS

Preface............................... I

PART I CHINESE RECIPES
PAGE

Rules for Cooking..................... 9
Soups................................ 12
Gravy............................... 19
Fish................................. 20
Poultry and Game.................... 27
Meats............................... 36
Chop Sueys.......................... 41
Chow Mains.......................... 47
Fried Rice........................... 51
Omelettes........................... 54
Vegetables.......................... 57
Cakes............................... 64

PART II JAPANESE RECIPES

Soups............................... 71
Fish................................. 75
Poultry and Game.................... 79
Omelettes and Custards............... 87
Vegetables and Relishes............... 93
Cakes, Candies, Sweetmeats...........104
Bean Sprouts and Beverages 109
List of Chinese and Japanese Groceries . . 111
Index...............................113

PREFACE

Chinese cooking in recent years has become very popular in America, and certain Japanese dishes are also in high favor. The restaurants are no longer merely the resort of curious idlers, intent upon studying types peculiar to Chinatown, for the Chinese restaurants have pushed their way out of Chinatown and are now found in all parts of the large cities of America. In New York they rub elbows with and challenge competition with the finest eating palaces. Their patronage to-day is of the very best, and many of their dishes are justly famous.

There is no reason why these same dishes should not be cooked and served in any American home. When it is known how simple and clean are the ingredients used to make up these Oriental dishes, the Westerner will cease to feel that natural repugnance which assails one when about to taste a strange dish of a new and strange land.

PREFACE

Bread, butter, and potatoes are never used by the Chinese or Japanese. Tea is drunk plain, with neither cream nor sugar, but great care should be used in its brewing. Rice is indispensable, and should be cooked in that peculiarly delectable fashion of which the Oriental peoples alone are past masters. The secret of the solid, flaky, almost dry, yet thoroughly cooked rice lies in the fact that it is never boiled more than thirty minutes, is covered twenty minutes, never stirred nor disturbed, and set to dry on back of range when cooked, covered with a cloth. Mushy, wet, slimy, overcooked rice is unknown to the Chinese and Japanese. Sweetened rice, as in rice pudding and similar dishes, is unknown. Rice takes the place of such staples as bread and potatoes. Syou, sometimes called Soye, is similar to Worcestershire and similar European sauces. In fact, the latter are all said to be adaptations of the original Chinese syou, and most of these European sauces contain

2

syou in their makeup. It lends a flavor to any meat dish, and is greatly esteemed by the Oriental peoples.

In China, with the exception of rice, bonbons, and so on, food is served in one large dish or bowl, out of which all eat, using the chopsticks. Considerable etiquette governs the manner of picking desired morsels from the main bowls. In high-caste or mandarin families a servant has his place at the foot of the table, but he stands throughout the meal. It is his duty to serve at the table the portions from the main dishes to each individual, and to do what the host generally does for the comfort of those at table. The other servants waiting on table take their orders from him, and he is really there as a sort of proxy for the host.

In Japan, individual meals are brought in on separate trays to each person. All sit cross-legged upon the floor before their trays. The Japanese consider it gross and vulgar to put food in quantity upon the plate. The portions are very small, the largest being about the size of an egg. There is a striving for daintiness and simplicity.

For this book only such Chinese and Japanese dishes have been selected as would appeal to the Western palate, and which can be prepared with the kitchen utensils of Western civilization. Many dishes prepared by the Chinese cooks in this country are only modifications of their native dishes. Recipes for the same dish, obtained from different parts of China, vary considerably. The combinations here given are those which experience has proved most easily prepared and most palatable.

The authors advise any one who intends to cook "Chinese" to go to some Chinese restaurant and taste the various dishes he desires to cook. A good cook always should know what a dish tastes like before he tries to cook it. All cooks can tell how the taste of a strange dish reveals to him

many things, and it is often possible
to guess of what the dish is composed.

No cookbooks, so far as the authors
know, have ever been published in
China. Recipes descend like heir-
looms from one generation of cooks to
another. The recipes included in this
book (the Chinese ones, that is) have
been handed down from Vo Ling, a
worthy descendant of a long line of
noted Chinese cooks, and himself head
cook to Gow Gai, one time highest
mandarin of Shanghai. They are
all genuine, and were given as an
especial expression of respect by a
near relative of the famous family of
Chinese cooks.

PART I

CHINESE RECIPES

RULES FOR COOKING

GENERAL

The first and the most important rule for Chinese cooking is cleanliness, first of the hands, second of the utensils, and third of the food.

Meat should not be washed, but should be rinsed in cold or lukewarm water and, if necessary, singed over a hot flame and scraped with a sharp knife.

All vegetables and fruit should be washed in cold water,—if necessary, in fifty different waters.

Never use soap to wash saucepans. Use washing soda or sand.

All cloths and dish towels should be boiled and rinsed thoroughly.

Care must be taken to measure accurately the ingredients of recipes, for the spices and relishes used in Chinese kitchens are exceedingly hot and pronounced in flavor.

To make rich stock for soup use

only a quart of water to every pound of veal, mutton, or beef bone.

To determine whether a fish is fresh, watch that its flesh is firm and thick, its scales glistening, and its eyes prominent.

When dropped into a bowl or pan containing cold water, eggs that are absolutely fresh will immediately sink to the bottom and rest there; eggs which are not perfectly fresh will stand on end or rise a little.

Delicious dishes can be obtained only from the use of the purest and best quality of ingredients. A good cook needs to be as well a discriminating purchaser.

Glass measures recording pints and quarts of liquid and ounces and pounds of solids (like sugar), with the fractions thereof, are handy and sanitary.

TO BOIL RICE

Use an iron pot. Wash the rice thoroughly in many waters, until, in fact, the water is as clear as for drinking. To one cupful of rice add

10

one and a quarter cupfuls of cold water. Cover tight, and boil slowly half an hour—no more. On no account stir. Rice should not be disturbed till it is taken up; that is the secret of the dry, finely cooked Chinese rice. Set on back of range, covered with a clean cloth or napkin, until ready to serve. Rice should be served in individual bowls, replenished as soon as empty throughout the meal. With the Chinese it takes the place of bread or potatoes. Salt is not added until it is served.

TEA

The quantity of tea used depends on the quality, and the taste of the individual. Rinse the pot with boiling water before putting in the tea. The water should just come to a boil—no more. Pour on the tea leaves. Let it stand for two or three minutes, but on no account must it be allowed to boil. Strain tea from leaves, and serve pure, if Chinese tea is used. See more about tea on page 109.

11

SOUPS

YEA FOO MAIN

One quart of soup stock; one quarter pound of mushrooms; three stalks of celery; one eighth clove of garlic; six water chestnuts; one quarter pound of vermicelli; one and one quarter teaspoonfuls of salt; one teaspoonful of syou (Chinese sauce).

Have the soup stock boiling hot. Then wash thoroughly in cold water all the above vegetables, and cut in small pieces. Add to the soup one tablespoonful of syou, and the salt and pepper. Let all boil twenty minutes; then add the vermicelli and boil fifteen minutes more. Serve with hard-boiled eggs cut in quarters.

YAT KO MAIN

One quart of soup stock; one quarter pound of noodles; one and one half teaspoonfuls of salt; one quarter pound of minced ham; one tablespoonful of syou; one small onion; one stalk of celery.

Boil the noodles until tender—about ten minutes. Then remove from the hot water, and put in cold water to soak, while preparing the soup. To one quart of good soup stock add one onion and one stalk of celery, chopped fine, pepper and salt, and one tablespoonful of syou. Boil ten minutes. Remove noodles from the cold water, add them to the soup, and boil for five minutes more. The ham should be shredded. Just before serving sprinkle it on top.

SOUP STOCK

Save all beef, veal, and chicken bones and clean pieces of meat; also the feet of chickens and the giblets. Wash the chicken feet and skin them, by first scalding in boiling water. Cover all the above with cold water and let it boil from five to eight hours slowly, with salt to taste. Drain liquor from bones, and set away to cool. When cold it will be a thick jelly, and is used as the foundation for various soups and gravies.

MO KU GAI T'ONG
(Spring Chicken Soup with Mushrooms)

Two and one half pounds of chicken; one quarter pound of lean pork; one quarter pound of dried mushrooms; one dozen lotus seeds; three stalks of celery; one teaspoonful of salt; one tablespoonful of syou; one onion.

Clean a fresh young chicken of about two and one half pounds. Cut off all the flesh; put the bones, with liver and gizzard, into three pints of cold water, and boil for two hours, adding water if it boils away. While the stock is boiling, prepare the following: Cut up the chicken meat into small pieces. Cut up very fine one quarter pound of lean pork. Wash and soak in lukewarm water one quarter pound of dried mushrooms. Pull off all the stalks. Peel and cut a dozen lotus seeds or water chestnuts. Chop three stalks of celery

14

very fine, and also one onion. Pour
off the liquor from the bones, and
strain. Cut up liver and gizzard fine
and return to stock. Add all the
ingredients, with one teaspoonful of
salt and one tablespoonful of syou.
Boil all together for one hour.

GAI GRUN YUNG WAA
(Bird's-nest Soup)

One half pound of bird's nest; one
pint of chicken stock; one quarter
pound of cooked breast of chicken; one
boiled egg; one quarter pound of
minced ham; one teaspoonful of salt.

To make this soup, the bird's nest
is first boiled an hour, then drained and
put into cold water. Meanwhile the
cooked chicken meat is well pounded,
so as not to be in large or hard pieces,
and a cupful of the cold stock is added
to it. Next the bird's nest is taken
from the cold water and well drained,
and added to the soup stock. Boil
for half an hour. Now the chicken
meat is added. and also the egg, the
latter having previously been finely

15

crumbled. The soup is taken off the fire as it begins to boil again after the last addition. Before serving, the minced ham is sprinkled on top.

Bird's nest is a gelatinous substance, a species of seaweed, with which certain Chinese birds, the esculent swallow and the white-backed swallow, build their nests. It is also found in Java. It is one of the most delicious of Chinese foods, and esteemed and praised not alone by the Chinese but by all travelers in the Orient.

SEAWEED SOUP

Two yolks of hard-boiled eggs; one can of seaweed; three chicken giblets; two tablespoonfuls of syou; one and one half teaspoonfuls of Quong Sang Chong (water chestnut flour).

Boil one can of seaweed until it is like thin jelly. Have ready three chicken giblets, chopped very fine, having first boiled them one hour in a quart of water. Add the seaweed, and boil all together for half an hour. Strain, then crumble in the yolks of

16

two hard-boiled eggs, stir in two
tablespoonfuls of syou, and salt to
taste. Rub smooth one and a half
teaspoonfuls of Quong Sang Chong in a
little cold water, then add to the soup
and stir until it thickens slightly.
Serve with a small piece of seaweed on
top that has been soaking in spiced
vinegar.

BÄK TOY GUN
(Chinese Soup of White Vegetables)

Two tablespoonfuls of syou; one
half pound of white mushrooms; one
dozen water chestnuts; one quarter
pound of bean sprouts; one stalk of
celery; two small onions; three eggs;
bit of garlic.

No meat or stock is used for this
soup. Have ready three pints of
boiling, salted water, with the two
tablespoonfuls of syou in it. Add
all of above vegetables (which have
been previously washed in cold water
and cut in small pieces) except the
mushrooms and celery. Boil for
fifteen minutes, then add the mush-

rooms and celery. Whip up the three eggs in a little cold water, and drop slowly into the boiling soup, stirring the soup as it drops, and it will form into fanciful shapes. Remove at once, and serve.

GRAVY

Use pork fat cut up and fried crisp. Then rub smooth one tablespoonful of Quong Sang Chong (water-chestnut flour) or rice flour in cold water, and stir it slowly into the boiling fat until it thickens and browns. Add syou, salt, pepper, and a little sugar. In preparing chop sueys and similar dishes, use this gravy if the mixture is too dry.

GRAVY WITH ONIONS

Place two tablespoonfuls of chicken fat or pork fat in pan, and when it is very hot add a finely chopped onion and fry a golden brown. Now slowly stir in one tablespoonful of flour until brown (taking care not to burn), salt, pepper, and a little sugar, then slowly pour boiling water, stirring all the time, until you have a smooth, rich gravy. Use for addition to the various dishes.

FISH

TEN SUNE GUNE
(Sweet and Sour Fish)

Two pounds of sea bass; one and one half cupfuls of water; one tablespoonful of Quong Sang Chong (waterchestnut flour); two and one half tablespoonfuls of vinegar.

Clean a sea bass of about two pounds. Take out all the insides, taking care to keep the fish whole. Then put it into a medium deep dish large enough to fit the fish. Pour over it water almost boiling, cover fish well over. Put a lid on dish, and leave on range for one hour. Do not boil, but keep it hot. Now prepare the following sauce: Rub smooth one tablespoonful of Quong Sang Chong. To a cup and a half of water add one tablespoonful of salt, one and one half tablespoonfuls of sugar, and two and one half tablespoonfuls of vinegar. Mix well. Boil until it thickens, stirring constantly to prevent burning. Dish up the fish, place on another hot, dry dish, then pour over it the sauce, and serve with rice.

PINEAPPLE FISH

Two pounds of fish; one tablespoonful of syou; one can of preserved pineapple.

Clean a haddock or codfish of about two pounds and take out the bones. Rub well with salt, and set in a fish pan. Cover well with boiling water, and let it simmer gently for twenty minutes. Drain off all the water, and add one tablespoonful of syou and one can of preserved pineapple. Let this simmer slowly for fifteen minutes longer. Thicken with cornstarch or Quong Sang Chong, and serve with rice.

LOBSTER OMELETTE

One teaspoonful of peanut oil; two eggs; one tablespoonful of cold water; one tablespoonful of chopped lobster meat; salt and pepper.

21

Use small frying pan and put into it a tablespoonful of peanut oil. Heat it. Now beat two eggs with a table-spoonful of cold water. Pour half in the pan. Have ready the cooked lobster, broken into small pieces. Quickly pour in the other half of beaten eggs, and cook slowly for five minutes. Slip off pan without break-ing, and make two or three more omelettes in exactly the same way, or have several small frying pans and cook all at once, serving one omelette on top of another in a hot water-heated platter.

COLD PICKLED FISH

Two pounds of fish; one pint of vinegar; one pint of water; four red peppers; one tablespoonful of salt; one teaspoonful of sugar.

Any white fish can be used that is large enough to slice. Wash the fish, then wipe dry and lay it in an earthen dish. Mix together one pint of vinegar and one pint of water, and when boiling, pour it over the fish. Cut

up four red peppers, taking out the
seeds. Sprinkle the salt and sugar
over the fish, and then lay in the
peppers. Cover tight, and put away
for two hours. Then drain off all
vinegar and water. This dish is very
good served with bamboo shoots,
rice, or any kind of vegetable.

YEU
(Fish Cakes)

Two eggs; one cupful of fish meat;
two cupfuls of rice flour; two tablespoonfuls of peanut oil; one and one
half teaspoonfuls of salt; one quarter
pound of almonds.

Take any dried fish, and remove all
bones and skin. Then pound the fish
to a powder, and mix one cup of the
fish with a quarter pound of blanched
almonds, also pounded, two cupfuls of
dried and powdered rice flour, and
half a teaspoonful of salt. Beat the
whites of two eggs with a little cold
water, enough to make a thin paste.
Mix well all together. Roll very
thin, cut into cakes, and bake in a

23

hot oven in hot peanut oil for twenty minutes. Remove the cakes from the oil, and drain on paper in a slow oven until cakes are dry and crisp.

SHRIMP OMELETTE

One half cup of shrimp meat; five eggs; one cupful of mushrooms; two tablespoonfuls of sweet lard; salt and pepper.

Put the sweet lard in the pan, and when hot throw in the mushrooms, which have been first washed and cut small. Cook for five minutes, then add the shrimp meat, which has previously been cooked and flaked. Cook for two minutes more. Beat five eggs and throw in the pan, and cook for five minutes, taking care not to burn, but do not stir or shake the pan, save very gently. Slip omelette off pan without breaking, and with the mushroom and shrimp side up, or folded in two. Serve on a hot platter.

DRIED SHRIMP STEW

Two cupfuls of dried shrimp; one tablespoonful of rice flour; one teaspoonful of salt; a dash of cayenne pepper; one and one half tablespoonfuls of syou.

Soak the shrimps in cold water for half an hour, drain, and cover with cold water, add the cayenne pepper and syou, and boil slowly about one hour. Mix the rice flour with cold water to a smooth paste, and stir until it thickens. Serve with rice.

CURRY SHRIMPS

One onion; one tablespoonful of olive oil; one and one half teaspoonfuls of curry powder; one tablespoonful of syou; one cupful of boiling water; one tablespoonful of rice flour; one teaspoonful of salt; one and one half pounds of boiled shrimps.

Fry to a light brown in one tablespoonful of pure olive oil, one onion, chopped fine. Mix one and one half teaspoonfuls of curry powder with a little cold water to make a smooth

25

paste, and stir it in. Add a tablespoonful of syou, a cupful of boiling
water, a teaspoonful of salt, a dash of
cayenne pepper, and dust with rice
powder, stirring until it thickens.
Have ready a pound of cooked shrimps,
flaked, or white fish may be used instead. Simmer for five minutes, and
serve with rice.

POULTRY AND GAME
FRIED CHICKEN
(Chinese Style)

Two and one half pounds of chicken;
two tablespoonfuls of sweet lard; one
tablespoonful of syou; one half onion;
one teaspoonful of cornstarch or Quong
Sang Chong; one teaspoonful of salt.

Clean a young spring chicken, and
cut it into small pieces. Fry to a
golden brown in hot, sweet lard.
Serve with a brown gravy prepared as
follows: Boil the giblets until tender,
then chop very fine and return to
the liquor in which they were boiled.
Add a tablespoonful of syou and half
an onion chopped fine; boil for
ten minutes. Thicken with a teaspoonful of cornstarch or rice flour, and
pour over the chicken. Serve hot,
with rice.

SHU BOK AP
(Fried Squab)

Two squabs; olive or peanut oil;
two chicken livers; one small onion;

two tablespoonfuls of syou; one table-spoonful of Chinese almonds; one quarter pound of white mushrooms; one teaspoonful of salt; yolks of two eggs, hard-boiled.

Cut the squabs in pieces, not too small. Let the legs be separated from the body, also the wings, and cut the rest in four pieces. Singe off all hair and feathers. Wash in cold water, and wipe dry. Dip each piece of squab in dry flour, and toss in boiling olive or peanut oil. Cook until it is crisp. Drain off all fat, while preparing the following: Put one tablespoonful of olive oil in the pan, and when it is hot, place the chicken livers (chopped very fine) in the fat, add a small minced onion, two tablespoonfuls of syou, a table-spoonful of Chinese small almonds, blanched and chopped, and a quarter of a pound of white mushrooms, cut small. Fry for ten minutes, then pour into hot dish and place the squab on top, garnished with crumbled hard-boiled yolks of eggs.

28

ROAST SQUAB

One plump squab; two chicken
livers; one dozen fresh mushrooms;
one tablespoonful of Chinese almonds;
one tablespoonful of chicken fat; two
tablespoonfuls of syou; one teaspoonful of salt; one quarter small onion;
one teaspoonful of cornstarch.

Clean and singe a plump squab.
Rub inside and out with salt. Stuff
it with the following: A dozen mushrooms, peeled and cut small, a tablespoonful of almonds which have been
blanched and chopped fine, and a
little minced onion. Mix together,
and fill the squab. Now sew or skew
tight, and melt the tablespoonful of
chicken fat and pour it over the squab.
Place in a hot oven and roast for
half an hour, basting and turning
frequently. Make the gravy, meanwhile, by chopping fine two chicken
livers and frying them in a teaspoonful
of chicken fat. When very brown,
stir in a teaspoonful of cornstarch
until brown. Now add two tablespoonfuls of syou, and serve with
the squab.

STEAMED DUCK

Three and one half pound duck; one quarter pound of pork; one quarter pound of mushrooms; one quarter pound of water chestnuts; one quarter cup of barley; one and one half tablespoonfuls of syou; one teaspoonful of salt.

After the duck has been well cleaned, inside and out, cut down the breast, dry well, and rub it thoroughly with salt. Lay in a bowl, and then prepare the following filling: Take one quarter pound of pork, chopped fine; one quarter pound of mushrooms, cut small, and one quarter pound of water chestnuts, sliced thin. Boil one quarter pound of barley for ten minutes, adding half a tablespoonful of syou and a teaspoonful of salt. Mix together all of the above ingredients, fill the duck, and sew or skew it up. Steam for three hours, and serve with rice.

DUCK WITH HERBS

Three to four pound duck; one quarter pound of pork fat; one onion;

two stalks of celery; one lemon
peeling; one quarter clove of garlic;
two tablespoonfuls of syou; one tablespoonful of mixed spices; one cup of
stock; one dozen mushrooms; one
teaspoonful of salt; one tablespoonful
of parsley.

Drain and singe the duck. Wipe,
then thoroughly dry, inside and out,
with a clean, damp cloth. Line a
pan with small pieces of pork (fat).
Sprinkle the bottom with minced
onion, celery, grated lemon peel, and
the garlic, grated fine. Lay the duck
in and cover with a tablespoonful of
mixed spices, two tablespoonfuls of
syou, and a cup of rich stock. Set
over the fire and simmer for two
hours, basting often. Wash the mushrooms and turn them in, and cook all
together for ten minutes. Take up,
and thicken the gravy with cornstarch or rice flour. Lastly, toss in
the chopped parsley. Cut up the
duck in small pieces (not too small),
arrange on dish, pour the gravy with
the herbs around the duck, and serve
hot with rice.

BOO LOO GAI
(Pineapple Chicken)

One young chicken; one tablespoonful of sweet lard; one tablespoonful of syou; one can of preserved pineapple.

Wash and singe a young, fresh chicken and cut off all the flesh. Slice it, put a tablespoonful of sweet lard in the pan, and fry. Do not let it burn. Add the chicken, and fry brown. Add a tablespoonful of syou and a can of preserved pineapple, and cook slowly for fifteen minutes. Thicken the pineapple juice with a teaspoonful of Quong Sang Chong, and serve hot with rice.

SWEET AND PUNGENT CHICKEN

Three and one half pound chicken; one dessert-spoonful of salt; two tablespoonfuls of sugar; two cupfuls of vinegar; one half onion; one tablespoonful of sweet lard; two tablespoonfuls of syou.

Take a young chicken of about three and one half pounds. Clean and singe it, and remove all the bones.

Lay in a stone dish and over it pour
(enough to cover well) a mixture of
two cupfuls of boiling vinegar, a
dessert-spoonful of salt, and two tablespoonfuls of sugar. Cover, and put
away in a cool place for twenty-four
hours. Prepare a brown gravy by
chopping half an onion and frying it
a light brown in sweet lard or chicken
fat. Cut the chicken into quarters,
and put in a pan with two tablespoonfuls of syou. Simmer for half an hour
very gently. Serve with rice.

LYCHEE CHICKEN

Two pound chicken; one teaspoonful
of salt; one quart of lychee nuts; two
tablespoonfuls of syou; one half small
onion; two tablespoonfuls of sweet
lard.

Cut into small pieces a fresh young
chicken of about two pounds and rub
well with salt. Fry two tablespoonfuls
of sweet lard a very light brown. Add
two tablespoonfuls of syou, and cover
tight. Simmer for half an hour.
Have ready a quart of lychee nuts,

peeled and stoned. Add these to the chicken, with the minced onion, and cook slowly for twenty-six minutes. Serve with rice.

HOP HO GAI DIN
(Fried Chicken with Almonds or Walnuts)

Two and one half pound chicken; two tablespoonfuls of olive oil; one cupful of Chinese almonds; two stalks of celery; one teaspoonful of onion juice; two tablespoonfuls of syou; one quarter pound of white mushrooms.

Use only the breast of a young chicken, and cut it in small tubes. Fry to a golden brown in two tablespoonfuls of olive oil. Take a cupful of almonds or walnuts, blanched and chopped, and half a pound of small white mushrooms cut up small; to this add a teaspoonful of onion juice and two tablespoonfuls of syou. Turn all in with the chicken and simmer half an hour. Thicken with Quong Sang Chong, and garnish with a border of nuts.

34

CHICKEN WITH MUSHROOMS

One tablespoonful of sweet lard; two pounds of chicken; one onion; one pound of fresh mushrooms; one tablespoonful of syou; two teaspoonfuls of salt.

Put the lard in the pan, and have it boiling hot. Cut up a young chicken, and remove all the bones; then lay it in the fat, and cook to a golden brown. Mince the onion and add. Wash and cut up the mushrooms, and add with a tablespoonful of syou. Cook all slowly for fifteen minutes.

MEATS

PORK WITH GREEN PEPPERS

One and one half pounds of pork; two tablespoonfuls of syou; six green peppers; one onion; one teaspoonful of salt.

Cut the pork in strips about two inches long and half an inch thick. Wash the peppers, remove the seeds, and cut into small pieces; then add to the meat with two tablespoonfuls of syou, one onion chopped fine, and a tablespoonful of salt. Cover, and cook for ten minutes. Serve with rice.

CHINESE FRIED PORK WITH ONIONS

One pound of pork; two large onions; two tablespoonfuls of syou; one teaspoonful of salt.

Cut about a pound of fresh pork (not too fat) in tubes, and fry a light brown. Cut up two large onions and fry with the pork until all is brown,

then add the salt and two tablespoonfuls of syou, and fry very hot. This
is very tasty, and good served with
boiled rice.

PEPPER STEAK

One and one half pounds of beef;
two tablespoonfuls of beef suet; three
tablespoonfuls of syou; six green
peppers; one onion.

Take the upper cut of the round
of beef and cut into strips about two
inches long. Fry in the beef suet for
about four minutes, then add one
onion, cut fine. Have the green
peppers washed and the seeds removed,
and cut in small pieces. Turn in
with the beef, and add three tablespoonfuls of syou and some salt.
Cover tight, and let simmer for ten
minutes.

BEEF KIDNEY WITH CHINESE
MUSHROOMS

One beef kidney; one quarter pound
of dried mushrooms; one small onion;
one and one half teaspoonfuls of salt;

dash of cayenne pepper; two tablespoonfuls of chopped fat pork; three
tablespoonfuls of syou.

Soak the kidney for half an hour in
cold water with a handful of salt;
then cut in small pieces and fry in
pork fat. Wash a quarter of a pound
of dried mushrooms in lukewarm
water, pull off the stalks, and soak
for ten minutes. Add this to the
kidney, with one small chopped onion,
one and one quarter teaspoonfuls of
salt, and three tablespoonfuls of syou.
Cover tight, and boil very slowly
for one hour, adding boiling water if
it dries. Serve with rice.

FRIED BEEF WITH MUSHROOMS

One pound of beef; one pound of
mushrooms; one small onion; six
lotus seeds; two tablespoonfuls of
syou; one teaspoonful of salt; one
half pound of suet.

Use the upper part of the round,
or rump steak, cut in small pieces
(strips about two inches long). Chop
up the suet and fry out all the fat,

drain, and fry the beef in it good and brown. Add the onion and slice the lotus seeds. Cut up the mushrooms and turn in. Fry for about two minutes, then add two tablespoonfuls of syou and salt. Cover up tight, and let it simmer for fifteen minutes. Serve with rice.

FRIED RICE WITH CHICKEN AND MUSHROOMS

One pound of rice; one pound of cooked flesh of chicken; one pound of fresh white mushrooms; two stalks of celery; one onion; six water chestnuts; one tablespoonful of pork fat; two tablespoonfuls of syou; dash of cayenne pepper; one teaspoonful of salt.

Boil one pound of rice for twenty minutes. While this is boiling, prepare the following: Take one pound of cooked chicken and cut it in small pieces. Put a tablespoonful of pork fat in the pan, and when it is very hot turn in the chicken and fry for a few minutes. Then cut up two stalks of celery, one onion, and six water chestnuts, and add with the syou cayenne, and salt. Fry all for ten minutes, then place the rice in a platter and pour the above over it. Cover tight, and let it soak through the rice thoroughly. Then garnish with chopped parsley, and serve.

CHOP SUEYS

Breast of one and one half pound chicken; one tablespoonful of chicken fat; one pound of fresh mushrooms; one half bunch of celery; one dozen water chestnuts; two white onions; one half can of bamboo shoots; two pounds of bean sprouts; one and one half teaspoonfuls of salt; two tablespoonfuls of syou.

Cut in small pieces the breast of a young chicken of about one and one half pounds. Put a tablespoonful of chicken fat in a deep frying pan, and heat very hot, then put in the chicken and fry brown, stirring to keep from burning. Have ready the following ingredients: One pound of fresh white mushrooms, cut small; half a bunch of celery, chopped; a dozen water chestnuts, peeled and cut in slices; two white onions, and half a can of bamboo shoots, all sliced. Add all these to

41

the chicken, and cook for ten minutes. Now add two pounds of bean sprouts, and cook for another five minutes with two tablespoonfuls of syou and a dash of cayenne pepper. Simmer for five minutes longer, and serve with rice.

DUCK CHOP SUEY

Three or three and one half pound duck; one tablespoonful of duck fat; one and one quarter tablespoonfuls of syou; dash of cayenne pepper; two teaspoonfuls of salt; one cup of dried mushrooms; one bunch of celery; one half cup of small white onions; one dozen lotus seeds; one can of bamboo shoots; two pounds of bean sprouts.

Carefully wash the duck and remove the bones, then wipe dry and pound the meat until tender. Then chop up about a tablespoonful of duck fat, and fry. Remove all lumps of fat, leaving only the clear oil, and put in the duck meat, cut in small pieces. Fry to a golden brown. Add one and one half

42

tablespoonfuls of syou, a dash of cayenne pepper, and half a table- spoonful of salt. Cover, and let simmer for twenty minutes while preparing the following: Wash and soak for ten minutes one cup of dried mushrooms, pulling off all stalks and cutting small; cut up a bunch of celery small, and add a cupful of small white onions. Slice a dozen lotus seeds very thin, and half a can of bamboo shoots. Put all in with the duck and fry ten minutes; then add two pounds of bean sprouts and cook five minutes longer. Serve with rice.

GAR LU CHOP SUEY
(With Chinese Dried Mushrooms)

One half pound of pork; one half pound of beef; one quarter clove of garlic; one onion; one half bunch of celery; one dozen lotus seeds; one half can of bamboo shoots; one and one half pounds of bean sprouts; three tablespoonfuls of syou; one teaspoon- ful of salt; dash cayenne pepper.

Cut half a pound of pork (not too

4

fat) into small pieces, and fry to a nice golden brown. Chop into small pieces half a bunch of celery, and wash and soak half a pound of Chinese dried mushrooms, discarding the stalks. Chop up one onion, and a very small piece of garlic, chopped very fine. Season with three tablespoonfuls of syou. Salt, and add a dash of cayenne. Fry for ten minutes, then add half a can of bamboo shoots and fry for five minutes longer. Lastly, add one and one half pounds of bean sprouts, and cook all together for ten minutes. Serve with rice.

GAI YUK CHEE YUK
(Chicken and Pork Chop Suey)

One half pound of breast of chicken; one half pound of lean pork; three tablespoonfuls of sweet lard; one half pound of mushrooms; one half bunch of celery; one dozen lotus seeds; one half can of bamboo shoots; two pounds of bean sprouts; one and one half teaspoonfuls of syou; one half teaspoonful of salt; dash of cayenne pepper.

Take half a pound of chicken cut from the breast and half a pound of lean pork, and cut both into small pieces. Heat three tablespoonfuls of sweet lard; when it is well melted, put the above meat in the fat and fry until brown, stirring to keep it from burning. Have ready the following ingredients: One half pound of fresh or dried mushrooms which have been washed in lukewarm water (if dried mushrooms are used, soak them for ten minutes and pull off the stalks), half a bunch of celery chopped small, a dozen lotus seeds or water chestnuts peeled and cut into thin slices. Cut up one onion, also half a can of bamboo shoots and two pounds of bean sprouts. Wash all well and drain in colander. Put all these, except the bean sprouts, with the meat, and cook for ten minutes; now add the bean sprouts, one and one half tablespoonfuls of syou, a dash of cayenne pepper, and salt, and cook for five minutes. Serve with rice.

45

CHOP SUEY (PLAIN)

One and one half pounds of pork; one and one half pounds of veal; two onions; one dozen water chestnuts; one half can of bamboo shoots; two pounds of bean sprouts; three tablespoonfuls of syou; one half tablespoonful of salt.

Cut half a pound of pork in small pieces, and fry for three minutes. Cut up the veal and add it, frying for five minutes. Chop up two onions and half a bunch of celery into small pieces, slice thin a dozen water chestnuts and half a can of bamboo shoots, and turn into the pan with three tablespoonfuls of syou and half a tablespoonful of salt. Cook for ten minutes. Add the bean sprouts, and cook all together for five minutes. Serve with rice.

CHOW MAINS

MEAT CHOW MAIN

One quarter pound noodles; one quart peanut oil; one half dozen water chestnuts; one half pound of pork; one half pound of veal; two tablespoonfuls of syou; one half bunch of celery; one onion; one half pound of dried mushrooms; two eggs; one quarter pound of ham.

Into a quart of peanut oil put a quarter of a pound of noodles, and cook until crisp; then remove and drain. Meanwhile take one pound of pork, cut it in small pieces, and fry a golden brown. Cut up half a pound of veal, and fry with the pork for five minutes. Add two tablespoonfuls of syou and half a tablespoonful of salt to this, and let it simmer slowly, while preparing the following: Wash, and soak for ten minutes, half a pound of Chinese dried mushrooms, pulling off the stalks; half a bunch of celery,

cut small; also one onion, chopped
fine, and half a dozen water chestnuts,
sliced fine. Turn these in with the
meat and cook all together for five
minutes. Place the noodles on a
hot platter as a bottom layer, then
the meat and vegetables. Garnish
the top with threaded ham and the
crumbled yolks of two hard-boiled
eggs.

CHICKEN CHOW MAIN

Two eggs; one teaspoonful of salt;
one quart of peanut oil; one half
pound of noodles; four ounces of pork;
two pounds of chopped chicken; one
stalk of celery; one onion; one half
pound of fresh mushrooms; one half
pound of breast of chicken, shredded;
three hard-boiled eggs; two tablespoonfuls of syou.

Have the peanut oil boiling hot and
toss in the noodles. Fry until they
are crisp, then take them from the oil
and drain, while preparing the following: Take four ounces of fine
chopped pork and half a pound of

chicken meat, also chopped. Now
add two tablespoonfuls of syou and
one teaspoonful of salt. Cook all
for ten minutes. Lay the noodles on
a platter, forming a layer at the
bottom of the dish, and place the
vegetables and gravy on top of the
noodles. Add a layer of the shredded
chicken breast, lastly the yolks of
hard-boiled eggs, crumbled, as a
garnish. Serve very hot.

LOBSTER CHOW MAIN

One pound of lobster meat; two eggs;
one half pound of noodles; three
stalks of celery; one can of bamboo
shoots; one onion; one quarter pound
of mushrooms; one tablespoonful of
sweet lard; one quart of peanut oil;
three water chestnuts.

First boil the peanut oil and into it
throw the noodles, cooking until crisp.
Remove and drain, while preparing
following: Put teaspoon of sweet lard
into frying pan, and when hot turn in
half the lobster meat, which has
previously been cooked. (Canned

lobster will do as well.) Cook for a few minutes, then add the onion, mushrooms, and water chestnuts. The bamboo shoots are added last, and all fried for ten minutes. Take a hot platter, and place the crisp noodles as a layer at the bottom of the dish, and spread above ingredients on top. Then take the other half of the lobster meat, and place a layer on top. Garnish with shredded yolks of hardboiled eggs.

FRIED RICE
FRIED RICE WITH HERBS

Two cupfuls of boiled rice; one and one half teaspoonfuls of pork fat; three stalks of celery; one large onion; five water chestnuts; one teaspoonful of salt; dash cayenne pepper; two tablespoonfuls of syou.

Fry one large onion a light brown in one and one half tablespoonfuls of pork fat; chop up three stalks of celery very fine, and add five water chestnuts, sliced thin. Fry all a light brown, then take two cups of rice that has boiled for twenty-five minutes, or use cold rice if you have any on hand. Mix all together with salt and cayenne and syou, and fry for ten minutes, shaking and stirring constantly. Serve hot, garnished with any meat or fish, or alone. This is very tasty.

FRIED RICE WITH EGGS AND HERBS

Six eggs; one half pound of rice; one quarter pound of pork, very fat; three water chestnuts; one stalk of celery; one onion; one teaspoonful of chopped parsley; one teaspoonful of salt; pinch of pepper.

First wash the rice and boil for half an hour. Cut up the pork very small, and fry brown. Add one onion, chopped fine; the three water chestnuts, sliced thin, and one stalk of celery, cut small. Salt and pepper, and fry all for ten minutes, taking care not to brown. Now turn in the rice, and fry five minutes. Meanwhile beat up six eggs, pour them over the mixture, stirring and shaking the pan constantly for five minutes, and serve hot.

FRIED RICE WITH TOMATO SAUCE

One teaspoonful of chopped parsley; two cupfuls of boiled rice; four tomatoes, or half a can; one onion; one tablespoonful of fat pork; dash of cayenne.

FRIED RICE

Cut up the pork and fry brown. Put in the onion, then the tomatoes and salt and cayenne. Fry for five minutes. Turn the rice, which has previously been cooked, into the pan and fry all together for five minutes. Place on hot platter, and garnish with minced parsley and eggs, threaded. Serve very hot. Make eggs thread by beating them with a tablespoonful of water, then pour through a sieve into boiling water and use as a garnish.

OMELETTES

FOO TAY DÄN
(Chinese Ham and Eggs)

Six eggs; one tablespoonful of ham
fat; one half cup of minced ham; one
half dozen water chestnuts; one half
of a small onion.

Heat one tablespoonful of ham fat
very hot. Chop up half a cupful of
ham meat; slice thin half a dozen
water chestnuts and half a small
onion. Fry all together for five
minutes; then beat six eggs, turn in
pan, and scramble.

FOO YUNG DÄN
(Chinese Omelette with Herbs)

Four eggs; one half a minced onion;
four sticks of celery; four ounces of
pork; one dessert-spoonful of syou;
one half teaspoonful of salt.

Beat four eggs well; have ready half
a minced onion and four sticks of
celery, chopped very fine. Put in
the frying pan four ounces of pork,

54

chopped fine, and fry until brown.
Now add the herbs, with a dessert-
spoonful of syou, and finally the
beaten eggs. Let the whole cook for
five minutes, without touching, but be
careful to keep it from burning. Fold
one half over the other, and slip on
the platter. Serve at once, with rice.

CHINESE SCRAMBLED EGGS

One half teaspoon of sweet lard; one
onion; five eggs; one teaspoonful of
salt; dash of cayenne pepper or black
pepper.

Put half a tablespoonful of lard in
frying pan and when it is very hot toss
in one onion, chopped fine, and fry
to a golden brown. Break five eggs
in a bowl, beat well, and turn into the
pan; then keep stirring until it is done.
It should all be a light golden brown.
This is very good with rice.

MUSHROOM OMELETTE

One tablespoonful of lard; one
quarter of an onion; one half pound of
fresh mushrooms; one tablespoonful

of syou; four eggs; one quarter tea-spoonful of salt.

Into a tablespoonful of hot, sweet lard fry quarter of an onion a light brown. Cut half a pound of fresh mushrooms very fine, and cook for five minutes. Beat four eggs with one tablespoonful of syou, and turn into pan. Cook for five minutes without touching, but keep from burning by gently shaking the pan. Fold over, or slip from pan into dish which is kept warm over a dish of hot water.

VEGETABLES

FRIED BEAN SPROUTS

Into a hot iron pan put a quarter of
a pound of fresh pork fat, and fry
brown. Drain all water from a pound
of bean sprouts, put into the hot fat,
and fry uncovered for five minutes,
stirring to keep from burning. Now
add to the three tablespoonfuls of
syou, salt, and pepper. Cover tight,
and let simmer for fifteen minutes.

FRIED CABBAGE

Wash and dry the cabbage, then cut
in long, slender strips, and throw into
a deep frying pan containing two
tablespoonfuls of hot fat. Sprinkle
with salt and pepper to taste and fry,
stirring for five minutes, shaking the
pan to keep cabbage from burning.
This is very good with rice, and is
used by the poor Chinese as a sub-
stitute for fish.

ENDIVE

Have water boiling hot and salted.
Now put in a tiny piece of washing
soda. Wash the endive, throw it into
boiling water, and boil slowly for ten
minutes. While boiling, take one
tablespoonful of olive oil and heat it.
Add one tablespoonful of vinegar, a
dash of cayenne, half a teaspoonful of
sugar, a teaspoonful of salt, and one
clove of garlic, chopped very fine.
Let this all simmer for five minutes,
then drain off the water, and pour
out the endive, and serve.

Endive is also good cooked as
follows: Place one tablespoonful of
sweet lard in pan, wash endive, and
fry it for five minutes. Then cover it
up tight and let it simmer in its own
juice for ten minutes.

CHINESE PICKLED YELLOW TURNIPS

Cut the turnip in thin slices, then
cut each slice in narrow strips until it
looks like strands. Place in bowl and
over it pour two cupfuls of vinegar,
a dash of cayenne, a quarter of a clove

of garlic, two teaspoonfuls of salt, and one teaspoonful of ginger, and let stand twenty-four hours before serving. To the above quantity use enough turnip for the vinegar to cover evenly.

EGG PLANT

One large egg plant; two cups of vinegar; one dessert-spoonful of mixed spices; one cup of sugar.

Cut one large egg plant in slices (not too thin). Soak for two hours in cold water with a handful of salt. Then drain this off, and pour over the egg plant a little vinegar mixed with water, and let it lie in this for about half an hour. Then drain thoroughly and pour over it two cupfuls of hot vinegar with dessert-spoonful of mixed spices and one cup of sugar. Cover tight and put away for at least twenty-four hours.

BOILED AND DEVILED CUCUMBERS

Peel the cucumbers, and place in salted boiling water. Boil slowly until the cucumbers become transparent.

Drain off all water and serve with a sauce made of one tablespoonful of olive oil and one teaspoonful of vinegar, beaten well with a dash of cayenne and the yolks of two hard-boiled eggs.

Cucumbers can also be cooked by placing one tablespoonful of oil or fat in a deep frying pan, and into this putting the washed and peeled cucumbers, rolling them about, and frying for five minutes. Cover tight, and let simmer in their own juice until transparent.

FRIED BAMBOO SHOOTS

Take one can of bamboo shoots and drain off all water. Wipe the bamboo shoots dry, and slice in long thin strips. Have ready boiling peanut oil, and toss the shoots into that. Cook until crisp. Delicious. Must be eaten hot.

WATER CHESTNUT SALAD

Peel and wash these little nuts, which are about the size of an ordinary chestnut. Slice very thin. Make a dressing of the following: To two tablespoonfuls of olive oil add the juice of one onion, one tablespoonful of fine vinegar, two teaspoonfuls of syou, one teaspoonful of salt, the yolks of two hard-boiled eggs crushed smooth, and half a teaspoonful of sugar. Mix all until smooth, then pour it over the water chestnuts. Sprinkle with chopped parsley.

CHAR QUÄ
(Chinese Artichokes)

Six char quars; one teaspoonful of olive oil; one tablespoonful of Quong Sang Chong; two tablespoonfuls of syou; two tablespoonfuls of chopped parsley; yolks of two hard-boiled eggs.

These little vegetables are peculiar to China, but are also grown very successfully on Long Island by the Chinese farmers. They have a very delicate flavor, and cooked the following way are very delicious, as well as extremely attractive. First wash thoroughly in cold water, then turn them into boiling salted water and boil about twenty minutes, meanwhile preparing the following sauce: Mix one teaspoonful of olive oil with one tablespoonful of Quong Sang Chong (water chestnut flour) until very smooth, then pour enough boiling water over it to make a thick cream. Add one teaspoonful of syou, and let it just come to a boil, stirring in the chopped parsley gently. Arrange the artichokes on a small platter with green lining, or place a green leaf under each artichoke. Fill the center of each with the yolks of hard-boiled egg, whipped smooth with a little olive oil and salt. Lastly, pour the sauce over, and serve. This should look like a water lily.

CHINESE FRIED PEAS
(Used by Children as Salted Peanuts are Used in America)

Put a teaspoonful of peanut oil in the frying pan, taking care to have one with a long handle, as the peas may pop. Toss a pint of yellow whole peas in the pan, and shake the pan while the peas roll about and turn a light brown. Chinese children make little cornucopia paper bags into which to put these peas and eat them like nuts.

PUMPKIN AND YELLOW SEEDS

Remove large seeds and spread them on paper. Sprinkle with salt, and bake them until dry.

FRIED NOODLES

Have about two quarts of boiling peanut oil. Throw in the noodles and fry a golden brown. Remove from oil, and drain off all fat by laying noodles on bit of paper.

CAKES

ALMOND CAKES

Two cupfuls of rice flour; one quarter cupful of almond oil; one half cupful of chopped almonds; one and one half cupfuls of powdered sugar; two eggs.

Mix thoroughly two cupfuls of rice flour, one and one half cupfuls of powdered sugar, and half a cupful of blanched almonds, chopped very fine, with a quarter of a cupful of almond oil. Moisten with two beaten eggs. Use no water, and if too stiff, add more egg. Roll about quarter of an inch thick, and cut in fanciful shapes. Place half an almond in the center of each cake, and bake them for one hour in a moderate oven. These cakes are certain to keep for a long time if they are placed in a tin box.

CAKES

GUM LU
(Golden Cakes)

One and one half cupfuls of rice
flour; one cupful of honey; one quarter
cupful of mixed nuts, chopped; three
teaspoonfuls of clarified goose fat;
yolks of two eggs; pinch of salt.

Take one and one half cupfuls of
rice flour and a pinch of salt and
into this work three teaspoonfuls of
clarified goose fat. Then chop very
fine about quarter of a cup of minced
nuts. Beat the yolks of two eggs,
and mix all together. Now pour in
one cup of raw, dark honey. If too
moist, add more flour. Stir thoroughly for fifteen or twenty minutes,
and pour into small cake pans, well
oiled, and bake slowly for two hours.

LAI YUT
(Beautiful Moon Tarts)

Two cupfuls of rice flour; one tablespoonful of clarified goose fat; two
eggs.

These tarts are a sort of dumpling.
Work a heaping tablespoonful of

clarified goose fat into two cups of rice flour. Add ice-cold water slowly to make a stiff paste. Roll out, brush with the whipped whites of eggs, and fold over several times, each time brushing with egg; then roll about quarter of an inch thick and cut into rounds about the size of a small saucer. Put in the filling, and place another round of paste on top. Press together at the edge, forming a rounded edge, and brush all again with white of egg. Bake for fifty minutes in a moderate oven, then remove the outer flake, which will leave the tart snow white. Decorate with a yellow moon in the center, cut from candied orange peel or painted with fruit coloring.

Filling: Two cups of lychee nuts, stoned and mashed to a pulp, one and one half cupfuls of sugar, quarter of a cupful of crystallized limes, and a teaspoonful of mixed spices. Mix all well together, and use to fill tart.

Another filling: Quarter of a pound of beef fat, cut in small pieces, one cupful of chopped dates, one cupful of preserved pineapple, quarter of a cupful of blanched chopped almonds, one and one half cupfuls of sugar, and one teaspoonful of mixed spices. Mix thoroughly.

PART II
JAPANESE RECIPES

SOUPS

SATSUMA SOUP

One small chicken; one medium-sized carrot; one pint of satorius (elephant-ear plant); two white radishes; one quarter pound of dried mushrooms; one quarter pound of aburage (oil-fried Tofu); one quarter pound of miso paste (soy bean and rice cheese); one half teaspoonful of mixed red-pepper spices.

To prepare the chicken, separate the meat from the bones; then put bones in cold water and boil slowly for about two hours. Strain, and add the well-chopped vegetables. (The mushrooms should have been washed, and soaked in lukewarm water for ten minutes previously.) Boil for one more hour, then add the chicken meat, cut in very small pieces, salt, spices, and half a teaspoonful of sugar. Cook all slowly for one hour. This makes about three pints of soup. It

is better to make it the day before it is
to be used. Soup is always improved
by standing over night. The late
Mikado took three or four sips of this
soup for breakfast.

TORI SHIRU
(Chicken Soup)

Two pound chicken (not necessarily
young); one half pound of egg noodles;
one half cupful syou sauce; one quarter
pound of white mushrooms; one half
dozen water chestnuts; salt, pepper,
and sugar.

Thoroughly clean and singe the
chicken, and scald feet to peel off
scabs or skin. Cut giblets in small
pieces and the chicken in about six
pieces, and cover with three quarts
of cold water. Boil all for about
three hours, according to the age of the
chicken. While it is boiling wash and
cut up the vegetables. Now make the
egg noodles of flour and eggs and roll
as thin as paper on a floured board,
then cut in shapes of flowers (chrysan-
themums, the Japanese prefer), and

leave spread out on the board to dry.
Drain all soup from the bones and
bring to a boil. Add vegetables,
salt, pepper, and one teaspoonful of
sugar; also the syou sauce. Boil all
for half an hour, then throw in the
noodles and cook for ten minutes.
Serve each bowl of soup with one
large noodle flower on top.

UWO SHIRU
(Fish Soup)

One and one half pounds of fish
(any kind); one quarter pound of fat
pork; one pound of miso paste (bean
and rice paste); one half cupful of
syou sauce; one cupful of cooking
juice sauce; one small carrot; two
onions; three hard-boiled eggs; two
tablespoonfuls of cooked, chopped
ham; pepper, salt, sugar, and spices.

To make this soup, any fish of the
milder variety can be used, such as
cod, haddock, or bass; lobster and
shrimps are also good cooked this
way. Have the pork cut into small
pieces, and fry a golden brown; then

73

wash the fish and take out all bones,
chop up into small pieces, add to the
pork, and fry for a few minutes.
Have ready all the vegetables, cleaned
and grated, and put into the pot
with the syou and cooking juice, salt,
pepper, and spices. Let it come to a
boil, then add the miso paste, mixed
with a pint and a half of boiling water.
Stir all well together, and boil for one
hour, adding boiling water if it cooks
away. Strain into soup bowls, and
serve with slices of hard-boiled eggs,
sprinkled with chopped parsley and
grated ham.

FISH

MUSHI KUJIRA
(Boiled Whale or Bass)

Two pounds of fish; one half teacupful of syou; orange and lemon skin; two long, large radishes; two tablespoonfuls of vinegar; salt, and dash of cayenne pepper.

Take off all bones and slice the fish daintily in long slices, and then in half-inch dice. Sprinkle with salt, and leave for about fifteen minutes. Cut radishes in long, even, delicate strips. Boil for a few minutes, strain, then add half a cupful of syou sauce and two tablespoonfuls of a fine vinegar. When it boils, drop in the fish slices. Boil up, then push to back of range, and, covered tight, let it simmer for half an hour. Grate the peels of half a lemon and half an orange, and sprinkle over the fish, after having removed it to a hot platter. Serve with boiled rice.

NOTE. This dish comes from Nagasaki, and is really a Japanized Chinese dish. Japanese cooking of fish greatly resembles that of the Chinese.

TEMBANI OF MACKEREL
(Fish Delicacy)

One good-sized mackerel; one fresh radish; one cupful of syou sauce; vinegar; orange or lemon peel; one half cupful of cooking juice.

Clean the fish, and remove all bones. Cut into half-inch dice; sprinkle with salt, and let stand for about half an hour. Wash the radish and cut into thin pieces, then throw it into the salted, boiling water. Boil for about five minutes, then strain off all water and add half a cupful of syou sauce and the same amount of cooking juice. Let all boil up, then add the fish and let it simmer for about twenty-five minutes. Remove from the fire, and before serving add a tablespoonful of vinegar. Place on a hot platter, and sprinkle with grated lemon or orange peel. Serve with boiled rice.

FISH

ONIGARA YAKI
(Broiled Lobster)

One lobster; syou sauce; salt and pepper; powdered sanshi spice.

Wash the lobster carefully in cold water. Place in boiling, salted water, and boil very slowly for one hour. Remove from the saucepan, and immediately throw into cold water. Cut in two pieces lengthwise, and dip each half in syou sauce. Place upon gridiron, and toast well both back and front, taking minute care not to blacken skin and fins. Once again cover with syou sauce, sprinkle with sanshi spice and pepper, and serve.

NOTE: Sanshi spice is made from the seeds that grow on the sanshi tree in Japan.

YAKI ZAKANA
(Fried Fish)

For any small fish. Wash the fish and scale it if necessary, removing all fins. Rub well with salt. Have ready a deep iron pot and use peanut or goma-seed oil, or, if preferred, olive oil. Do not have too much oil in pan, but only enough to prevent burning. Lay the fish in the pan, but do not crowd one on top of another; fry a light brown, being careful in turning not to break the fish. Have ready oil-fried Tofu, and place each fish on a cake of about the length of the fish. Sprinkle with grated lemon peel, and serve with rice, very hot.

NOTE: Tofu is made from a mixture of syou bean and rice. It is mashed and rolled into a thin cake, and fried in oil, very much like pancakes.

JAPANESE FISH BALLS

Take any boiled fish, cold, and mix with rice, boiled to a paste. Roll in flour to balls the size of large marbles; toss into boiling goma-seed oil, and fry a golden brown.

POULTRY AND GAME
YAKI UDZURA
(Broiled Quail or Pigeons)

Quail (or pigeons); mushrooms; aburage (bean cheese paste) Tofu; olive oil; parsley.

Prepare the quail or pigeons the day before using by washing and singeing and rubbing with salt, then put them away in cool place. Next day take half a pound of aburage, and fry the Tofu cakes in oil. Set in warm place to drain off the oil while toasting the birds. Dip the birds in olive oil, then in dry flour, and toast over a red-hot fire, turning quickly until they are a crisp brown. Place each bird, or half of a bird, if it is a pigeon, on the fried Tofu, and have some white mushrooms which have been fried in oil, placed around the birds. Then sprinkle with chopped parsley, and serve very hot.

79

SHIKA SHIRO
(Pot-roasted Venison)

Three pounds of venison steak; one cupful of syou sauce; one cupful of vinegar; two tablespoonfuls of sugar; one quarter pound of fresh pork (fat); one quarter pound of miso paste; one onion.

Place the meat in an earthenware bowl and cover with one cup of vinegar, two tablespoonfuls of sugar and the same amount of salt, one tablespoonful of mixed spices, and one onion, sliced. Cover, and put away to pickle for two or three days in a cool place. When ready to cook, remove meat from the juices, cut up the pork in small strips, and fry a light brown in deep iron pan. Add the venison meat, and fry well on both sides until brown, taking care not to burn it. Add the syou sauce, cover tight, and let simmer for one hour, or two, if necessary. Mix the miso paste with a little cold water, and stir it until it thickens. Remove the platter, and garnish with slices of lemon sprinkled with chopped parsley.

FRIED SQUAB

Take very small squabs, clean them,
and rub dry. Separate the legs and
wings, and cut the body into small
pieces. Toss into boiling peanut oil,
and cook until crisp. Remove, drain
off oil, and serve on fried Tofu.

HATO SHIRO
(Stewed Pigeon)

Two good-sized pigeons; one cupful
of syou sauce; one half cupful of
mirin sauce or sherry; one tablespoonful of sugar; one small onion;
two tablespoonfuls of kudze starch;
one quarter pound of fat fresh pork;
one dozen water chestnuts; one quarter
pound of bamboo shoots; salt and
pepper.

Select good, plump pigeons and
singe and clean thoroughly, then dry.
Rub well with salt. Take the fat
pork and fry out all the fat, and when
boiling hot put in the pigeons and
brown all over, rolling them on all
sides. Have ready the water chestnuts, washed and cut in thin slices,

also the bamboo shoots cut in thin strips. Chop up the onion very fine, and turn into the saucepan with the pigeons, adding the syou sauce, pepper, salt, and sugar. Cover very tight, and simmer over a slow fire for one hour. Then add the mirin sauce, or sherry. Lastly, mix two table-spoonfuls of kudzu starch in cold water, and stir into the juice until it thickens. Serve with rice.

MUSHI KIJI
(Roast Pheasant)

One good pheasant; one pound of small Japanese almonds; one and one half cupfuls of rice paste (comes prepared); three cupfuls of mirin sauce; one half cupful of cooking sauce; one tablespoonful of sugar; salt, pepper, and mixed spices; oil.

Wash and singe the bird, then rub well with salt. Place in deep dish and cover with three cupfuls of mirin sauce; more, if that quantity does not cover the bird. Lay away in a cool place over night, then drain off all liquid and have ready the almonds, blanched and chopped very fine. Add them to the rice paste with the sugar, a little salt, quarter of a cup of cooking sauce, and a pinch of mixed spices. Stir all together, and stuff the pheasant with this mixture. Sew up, and truss. Have ready boiling hot olive oil or goma-seed oil, pour it over the pheasant, and place in a hot oven. Roast until tender (about one hour), adding little by little the rest of the cooking sauce, and basting frequently. Cook for a half-hour longer, then place on hot platter and garnish with flower petals and water cress.

USAGI AMAI-SUI
(Hare, Sweet and Sour)

One good-sized rabbit or hare; one cupful of vinegar; one cupful of syou sauce; one tablespoonful of salt; three tablespoonfuls of sugar; one half cupful of mirin sauce; one tablespoonful of mixed spices; one half pound of fat fresh pork; one dozen red plums; one small lime or lemon.

Take a small hare or large rabbit
that has been hanging for at least two
days, and after it has been skinned,
and the insides removed, wash well
in cold water.   Cut in quarters and
put in a deep dish, covering it well
with the vinegar, sugar, salt, and so
on, mixed with water.   Add the spices
also, and a quarter of a cupful of
mirin sauce.   Cover up well, and let
it pickle in a cool place for two or
three days; then remove it from the
liquid and cut in small pieces.   Have
ready the fat pork cut in small pieces,
and fry.   Toss in the hare, and brown.
Now have ready a covered China cook
dish or casserole, and place in it the
hare and pork, adding the syou
sauce, a pinch of salt, pinch of the
spices, and the quarter cupful of
mirin sauce.   Cover up tightly, and
cook in a slow oven for one hour.
Then prepare a dozen large red plums,
removing the stones, and add them.
Dissolve one teaspoonful of Kanton
(Japanese gelatine) and mix with the
gravy, taking care not to break the

plums. Cook for another five minutes, then place on a hot platter, decorated with slices of lemon or limes, with a plum placed on top of each slice. This is good served either with white-bean cakes or rice.

MUSHI AHIRU
(Baked Duck)

Clean and singe the duck and wash in lukewarm water, then wipe dry with a clean cloth. Rub well with salt. Cut in pieces, and dip each piece of the duck in a batter made of kudzu starch and eggs. Make the batter of about the thickness of fritters. Lay these in a pan that has been oiled, and bake in a slow oven for two hours. Make a gravy by chopping the giblets very fine and putting them in a pot with a cupful of water, a cupful of syou sauce, salt and pepper, and a teaspoonful of sugar. Boil slowly while the duck is baking. Place the duck, which should be well browned, on a platter, then pour over it the gravy and garnish with orange or lemon peel, grated.

85

ROAST CHICKEN
(Japanese Style)

Take a young, tender chicken and clean and singe. Put the feet to boil until the scabs scale off, then place with the giblets to boil slowly. Make a stuffing of rice boiled dry in chicken gravy, add chopped onion and a pinch of mixed spices, salt, pepper, and a dash of cayenne. Put this in body of chicken and sew up. Roast for an hour, or longer, according to age of chicken. Make a gravy from the stock of the giblets. Chop the giblets up fine and add to the gravy. Serve with roasted sweet potatoes.

OMELETTES AND CUSTARDS

UNOHANA YAKI
(Flower Custard)

Two ounces of Kanton (Japanese gelatine); six eggs; three tablespoonfuls of cherry sirup; one ounce of goma seeds.

To make the pink custards, whip the whites of five eggs into the dissolved two ounces of gelatine. Add, while stirring over a slow fire, three tablespoonfuls of cherry sirup. Let it come to a boil, then pour quickly into flower-shaped molds, and let it set.

Yellow custards can be made by using the yolks instead of the whites of eggs, and half a pint of coconut milk. When the custards are solid, turn them from the molds on to large leaves on a plate, or decorate the flowered custard with leaves suitable to the flower represented. If the flower has a dark center, use goma seeds, and if variegated colors are

87

liked, pour half the yellow and half the cherry custards into the molds. The effect is very pretty, and the custards delicious. The pouring should be done very quickly and lightly, and the molds, of course, should be of flower designs. All travelers are enthusiasts on the subject of Japanese flower custards.

KINOKO-TAMAGO-YAKI
(Shrimp Omelette)

Four eggs; one half cupful of shrimp meat; one half cupful of syou sauce; goma-seed oil.

Beat up the eggs with half a cupful of syou. Have ready about four or five small frying pans. Wipe pans when hot with paper soaked in goma-seed oil. Pour into each pan an equal quantity of the egg, and quickly divide and scatter in the shrimp meat, which has been finely chopped. Fry all slowly for four minutes. The Japanese brown both sides at once, by putting some burning charcoal into a tin plate and laying this on top of the omelette on the stove. The omelette should be served very hot, and for this purpose there are special omelette dishes, Chinese and Japanese, the lower part of which is a hot water holder.

USU TAMAGO YAKI
(Fried Eggs)

One half dozen eggs; one cupful of cooking juice; two tablespoonfuls of syou sauce.

Beat the eggs with chopsticks, adding the cooking sauce and syou. Mix all well. Wipe a frying pan with paper soaked with goma-seed oil, and as soon as pan is well heated, pour in the above mixture and fry over a slow fire.

TAMAGO TOFU

Eggs; cooking juice; syou sauce; horseradish.

Break any required number of eggs and beat with chopsticks. Mix with twice the amount of cooking juice and one third of syou sauce. Pour

89

the mixture into a thin china bowl or
a tin mold, and steam over boiling
water for thirty or forty minutes.
Transfer a soupladleful to each
individual bowl, and over each pour
a small quantity of cooking juice and
a few drops of syou sauce. Sprinkle
with ground horseradish, and serve
very hot.

SCRAMBLED EGGS
(Japanese Style)

Eggs; green pepper; cold boiled
rice; mushrooms.

Break into frying pan half a dozen
eggs, stirring lightly with knife. Add
quickly, before egg begins to cook,
a tablespoonful of chopped green
pepper, the juice of an onion, half a
cupful of chopped mushrooms, and
half a cupful of boiled rice. Toss all
quickly together. Cook over a very
slow fire, and serve hot.

SAKURA
(Cherry Custard)

Beat up lightly and frothily six fresh
eggs. Add one cupful of milk, sugar,

90

and three tablespoonfuls of cherry
sirup. Throw a handful of ripe,
plump red cherries into the baking
pan, and over this pour the above
mixture. Bake for about half an hour
in a medium oven. Then remove, and
at intervals over top of dish set more
cherries. Sugar is unnecessary where
the cherries are sweet and ripe, as the
sirup will then suffice.

TAMAGO BOLAN
(Peony Eggs)

Boil five eggs hard. Place in cold
water. Remove shells carefully, so
as not to blemish whites. Carefully
cut off top with thread, one end
between teeth, the other between
fingers, drawing thread through egg.
Remove the yolks. Boil a small
pink snapper (fish) in hot water for
ten minutes, or steam for thirty.
Remove all bones and fins, and chop
together until fine. Mix with finely
mashed miso, pepper, and salt. Chop
yolks daintily and fluffily, and mix
with fish meat. Fill the whites with

7   91

this mixture. Now place the filled whites in center of a lettuce head and arrange fine strips of udo shoots round it. To fix lettuce head properly, all the leaves should be carefully adjusted and separated, washed, and then put back into shape again. It looks now like a bouquet, and is held together with toothpicks.

VEGETABLES AND RELISHES

KUWAI-KINTON
(Water Chestnut Cream)

Fifteen large water chestnuts; three quarters pound of sweet potatoes; three tablespoonfuls of vinegar; three quarters pound of sugar; one half pint of mirin sauce.

Peel the skin from fifteen large water chestnuts and slice them very thin. Boil in lukewarm water for about fifteen minutes. Peel the sweet potatoes, cut in slices, and dip in ice-cold water three or four times, changing the water with each dipping. Boil about one quart in an enameled saucepan, add the vinegar, then throw in the sweet potatoes. Cover, and boil for about twenty minutes; then, if tender, drain off all the water and add the sugar, with five table-spoonfuls of warm water and also the mirin sauce. Add a pinch of salt. Then place over the fire and add the above prepared water chestnuts.

When the water chestnuts have thoroughly absorbed the juice, add the strained sweet potatoes, stir with wooden spoon, taking care not to burn it, and boil until it is firm. Serve hot or cold—it is better hot.

MUSHI TAMANA AND BUTA
(Cabbage and Pork)

One good-sized hard cabbage; one cupful of syou sauce; one tablespoonful of sugar; one pound of salt pork; one onion; salt and pepper.

First boil the salt pork for one hour, then chop it in small pieces. Select a good hard cabbage without blemishes and wash it thoroughly in cold water; soak it in water with a handful of salt to kill all possible vermin. Remove from salted water, and rinse in fresh water, removing all salt. Carefully cut out the heart and center leaves, making a good-sized pocket, and fill this space with the chopped pork and one onion chopped very fine, salt, pepper, and a teaspoonful of goma seeds. Press the cabbage

94

leaves back into place, and tie tight in cheesecloth. Have ready a deep pot of boiling salted water, and in this place the cabbage in the bag. Cover, and boil slowly for two hours. Remove to a platter, and pour over it the syou sauce, which has first been boiled. Serve with rice.

SHIRO URI
(Stewed Squash)

These squash or various kinds of vegetable marrows are best simply peeled and boiled in salted water for twenty minutes, then removed and allowed to simmer in boiling syou sauce for five minutes longer. They are also very good stuffed with chopped meat or fish. To stuff one, take cold meat, chop it very fine, then mix with it two tablespoonfuls of miso and salt, pepper, and spices, and two tablespoonfuls of syou, and fill the center. Fish can be used instead of meat; but if fish is used, add the juice of a lemon.

95

NASUBI YAKI
(Fried Eggplant)

Peel the eggplant and cut it in slices.
Cover with ice water and a handful of
salt. Put on a heavy weight, iron or
stone, to press out the juice, and
leave for about half an hour. Then
strain off all water, which will be a
dark brown, and rinse with fresh cold
water, wiping dry each slice. Dip
each piece in beaten eggs, and fry in
goma-seed oil; drain off all oil. Place
on a platter, covering well with one
cupful of cooking sauce, boiled.
Sprinkle with goma seeds, and serve
with rice.

AMAI TAMANA
(Sweet and Sour Cabbage)

Cut a small, hard cabbage very fine.
Place in frying pan one tablespoonful
of goma oil, and when it is boiling hot
throw in the shredded cabbage.
Sprinkle with salt, and fry, stirring
constantly to keep it from burning.
Add one tablespoonful of sugar, the
same quantity of vinegar, and a little

piece of lemon or orange peel, shaved very fine. Cover tight, and let all simmer for twenty minutes. Finally add half a teaspoon of goma seeds. Serve hot.

SATSUMA TAMANA
(Cabbage, Satsuma Style)

Wash and shred fine a hard, crisp cabbage. In deep pan put goma-seed or olive oil. Add the cabbage, with half a dozen stoned prunes and the juice of a lemon, pepper, and salt. Let this slowly stew in its own juices for an hour or so. Raisins can be used instead of prunes, if preferred. It is a delicious way of cooking cabbage, the fruit lending a most delightful aroma to the cabbage.

FRIED CABBAGE

Wash and shred a hard cabbage. Put olive oil in deep iron pot, and add the cabbage, pressing down until it is absorbed into the oil and moisture. Add pepper, salt, and syou sauce, and let simmer slowly for half an hour.

Remove lid about ten minutes before serving, to allow cabbage to brown.

CHICKEN LIVER PASTE

Fry chicken livers over slow fire, or boil if preferred. Drain from water or fat when cooked, and crush through sieve. Fry a cupful of fresh or dried mushrooms. Crush these also through sieve, and add it to the livers. Add the juice of an onion and some lemon juice. Serve on salted crackers. Delicious for sandwiches.

GIBLET PASTE

Boil giblets until they are in shreds. Crush through sieve, then add the juice of an onion and lemon juice. Whip lightly with the hard-boiled yolk of eggs. Serve on crackers, with crumbled yolks of eggs sprinkled on top.

Pastes can also be made in a similar manner from soft meats and fish. Onion is usually added, and sometimes chopped parsley.

98

SUMOMO SUI AND AMAI
(Plums, Sour and Sweet)

Have a sirup made of half a cupful
of water, two cupfuls of sugar, a
quarter cupful of vinegar, and half a
teaspoonful of mixed spices, ground.
When it is boiling drop in the plums,
and let boil slowly for twenty minutes.
Add half a cupful of mirin sauce, or any
other desired spirits, and let all come
to a boil once. Remove, and serve.

BAKED BANANAS

Split the bananas on one side of the
skin. Place in a medium oven and
bake for about ten minutes. Now
take the fruit carefully from the skin,
taking pains not to break the skin.
Whip smooth with chopped dates and
almonds (about a teaspoonful of dates
and nuts to each banana), return mixture to shell, and serve with powdered
rice or sugar. Serve cold or hot.

STUFFED BANANAS

Bake long, plump bananas for ten
minutes in medium oven. Remove

and split skin down one side. Remove the inside, and whip it up with shredded coconut, a little cream and sugar, and a little lemon juice. Return to shell, and bake for another ten minutes.

TORI-KAN
(Chicken Jelly)

Two pounds of chicken flesh; one half pound of seaweed jelly or gelatine; one tablespoonful of sugar; salt and pepper; one quarter pound of dried mushrooms; one cup mirin sauce.

Cook in boiling water a young, tender chicken until it is tender. Take from the liquid, remove all the bone and cut in small pieces. Pick off stalks from mushrooms and soak in lukewarm water for twenty minutes. Cut in small pieces and boil for twenty-five minutes in about two cupfuls of water. Add the mirin sauce and boil again about five minutes. Wash the dry seaweed jelly and soak for about two hours, then take from water and squeeze dry. Break into small pieces and boil in one quart of water until it dissolves. Strain into another saucepan, with a pinch of salt and a tablespoonful of sugar. To this add the mushrooms and mirin sauce, and mix all together, with the chicken meat, salt, pepper, spices, etc. Have ready a lacquered box or smooth wooden box or mold, and pour in the mixture. Let it set, and, when serving, cut it in slices.

KAREFISH NIGORE
(Sole Jelly)

One medium-sized sole; one cupful of mirin sauce; two carrots; one quarter pound of dried mushrooms; one half pound of Kanton (dried seaweed jelly).

First prepare the sole by cutting away the head and thoroughly cleaning and scaling. Cut in fillets or slices, removing the small bones. Take one cupful of mirin sauce and a pinch of salt. Place in pot, and boil only a few minutes. Chop into small pieces two carrots and about a quarter pound

101

of dried mushrooms (first washed and
soaked). Boil in a small quantity of
water, and when tender, strain. Add
the mirin sauce, previously boiled for
fifteen minutes. Wash half a pound
of dry seaweed jelly, and soak in
water for two hours. Take out, and
squeeze dry. Break in small pieces,
and throw in pan with a quart of
water. Boil and dissolve. Strain into
another saucepan. Add half a cupful
of sugar and a tablespoonful of syou
sauce. With this mix the fish and
vegetables, and stir thoroughly.
Transfer to lacquered or smooth
wooden box, and let it set. When it
is firm, cut in desired small shapes.
Properly prepared, this is really delicious. It should be made the day
before it is to be served, as of course
it is eaten cold.

RINGO-KAN
(Apple Jelly, Japanese Style)

One half pound of seaweed jelly;
three quarters pound of sugar; two
big, tart apples; two tablespoonfuls of
kudzu starch.

VEGETABLES AND RELISHES

After washing half a pound of seaweed jelly soak it in water for about three hours, then squeeze it dry and break in small pieces into a pan with one and a half quarts of water. Boil over medium heat. Add three quarters of a pound of sugar, stirring the while, and a pinch of salt. Prepare two big, tart apples by peeling and removing the cores, then rub them on a nutmeg grater until they are reduced to powder. Transfer jelly to another saucepan, strain it, and mix with powdered apple. When thoroughly boiled, add two tablespoonfuls of kudzu starch, dissolved in cold water. Stir well with wooden chopsticks or spoon. Remove from fire, and pour into lacquered box or molds. Two or three hours after it has hardened, cut in desired shapes and sizes.

CAKES, CANDIES, SWEETMEATS
Chinese and Japanese

KATAMOCHI

This cracker comes ready prepared in boxes, and is good to serve with soups, oysters, etc. For those who wish to make it, the following recipe is given: Moisten the rice flour and allow it to rise of itself over night, no yeast or baking powder being used. Add salt, and roll into thin crackers. The process is precisely the same as the Jewish Matzoth cracker, and there appears to be a similarity also in the names, which has caused students often to point to it as another interesting evidence that the Japanese people are of Semitic origin — perhaps the "lost tribe"!

YOMOGA GA SHIMA

This crisp little Japanese cake also comes prepared in boxes. It acquired fame through its being the favorite cake of the late Mikado.

104

To make it, boil to a paste fresh or dried (previously soaked) lima beans. When they are cooked, set them aside to cool and thoroughly dry, then pound them to a fine flour. Roll on a floured board into thin crackers, and bake in a hot oven till crisp. They can be sweet or not, as desired.

Lily-root candy can be bought at almost any Chinese store. It has the consistency of very stiff gumdrops, and one variety, called Chicken Neck, is peppered over with red seeds.

SAN CHAR GO

A favorite Chinese candy, made from red Chinese dates.

The fruit is first mashed to a pulp, then mixed with powdered sugar and gelatine, beaten into a paste, rolled in sheets as thin as paper, and spread in the sun to dry. After it has dried crisp, it is cut into squares of six by four inches, wrapped in waxed paper, and packed in bundles. It has a delightfully piquant flavor, tart and sweet.

OWA OKASHI

A favorite Japanese candy. It is made of sweet rice, roasted over an open fire, same as popcorn, mixed with goma seeds, and held together in pressed bars with barley sugar. It is an improvement over the American popcorn-peanut balls.

YOHAN CANDY

Boil adzuki (purple beans) to a paste, and mix with sugar and seaweed gelatine. Allow it to harden.

CHESTNUT KINTONS
(Cream Candy)

One quart of chestnuts; one pint of sweet potatoes; one pound of sugar; three quarters pint of mirin sauce; one tablespoonful of vinegar.

Blanch the chestnuts and place them in lukewarm water. Boil, changing water several times, until you can pierce the nuts with a needle. Strain off water, then add one pound of sugar, three quarters of a pint of mirin sauce, and boil slowly. Have ready sweet potatoes which have been peeled and boiled for twenty minutes. Add to them the vinegar, and strain and press through sieve. Gradually mix with the chestnuts, and slowly boil, stirring constantly, until dry; then mold into desired shapes. Roll in powdered sugar.

This might be called the Japanese Fudge.

DAI-KAN
(Orange Jelly Candy)

One half pound of Kanton (seaweed jelly); three quarters pound of fine white sugar; three tablespoonfuls of kudzu starch; two oranges.

Wash half a pound of dry seaweed jelly, and soak it for two and a half hours in cold water. Then squeeze out all the water and break in small pieces. Boil in about a quart of water, until well melted, then mix three quarters of a pound of sugar with this, stirring with chopsticks or wooden spoon. Strain into another pan, and boil over medium fire. Take three tablespoon-

8

fuls of kudzu starch and dissolve in a little cold water. Then, drop by drop, gradually drop this into the jelly, while stirring with wooden spoon. When it becomes transparent, squeeze in the juice of two oranges and immediately remove from fire. Pour into a wooden box, and set in cool place for two hours to harden.

SWEET POTATO CANDY

This is loved by Japanese children, and is easily made. Boil sweet potatoes, mash and roll them into little balls, then toss into boiling sirup. Let them brown. Take out, and set to cool and become brittle.

RICE AND NUT CANDIES

These come in a great variety of ways. They are made chiefly of boiled rice pressed into balls with chopped nuts, tossed into boiling sirup, and then allowed to cool and harden. Seeds are often added, but these cannot be obtained in America.

BEAN SPROUTS AND
BEVERAGES

HOW TO PREPARE BEAN SPROUTS

These come in cans, but it is better to make them fresh at home, and it is easily done.

Take ordinary white beans, or dried lima beans, and soak over night in lukewarm water. In the morning take a large cloth, wet it, and set it on a table. Over this spread the beans. The cloth must be kept wet. In a night or two the beans will have sprouted. Use the sprouts as directed in the chop suey recipes.

BEVERAGES

Tea, of course, is the staple drink of both the Chinese and the Japanese, and it comes in any number of varieties. Of the Chinese teas a few may be especially recommended, such as Loong Taing, Long Gue, Oolong, and Lung Sue. Of the Japanese teas, Gyukura, or, in English, Pearl Dews,

tea is delicious. Coconut milk with
flower petals floating in it is another
favorite beverage. Chinese whisky
and wine are very strong, and have a
smoky flavor much appreciated by
the epicure. Saké, famous as chief
drink of the Japanese, is a sort of rice
wine, with a curious salty-sweet taste
to it. It is very good, when once
one becomes accustomed to it.

LIST OF GROCERIES
Chinese and Japanese

Almonds, Chinese
Apricots, green and red, crystallized
Apricots, green, preserved
Bacon, Chinese
Bamboo shoots
Beans and peas, various kinds of
Bean sprouts
Bird's-nest by box or pound
Carambola, crystallized
Carambola, preserved
Cherry blossoms, crystallized
Chicken neck
Duck, dried
Eggs, preserved
Fish, all kinds of
Fish, dried
Fruit, mixed, preserved
Ginger in sirup
Ginger, preserved
Ginger, sour pickled
Ginger, sugar, dried
Ginger, sweet pickled
Hams, Chinese

LIST OF GROCERIES

Honey candy
Kumquats, preserved
Lily-root candy
Limes, golden, crystallized
Limes, golden, preserved
Lotus seeds
Lychee nuts
Lychees, preserved
Melon and pumpkin seeds, salted
Mushrooms, canned
Mushrooms, Chinese dried
Mushrooms, fresh
Noodles, Chinese (all kinds)
Nuts, all kinds of mixed
Nuts, salted
Owa Okashi
Pineapple, preserved
Prunes, Chinese
Rice cakes, boxed, all kinds of
San Char go
Star fruit, crystallized
Sui Sin Fu candy
Syou (Chinese sauce)
Tofu (Japanese fried cakes)
Vegetables, fresh Chinese
Water chestnuts
Yohan candy

INDEX

Page

Preface............................ 1

PART I. CHINESE RECIPES
Cakes

Almond Cakes...................... 64
Golden Cakes (Gum Lu)............. 65
Gum Lu (Golden Cakes)............. 65
Lai Yut (Beautiful Moon Tarts)...... 65
Tarts, Beautiful Moon (Lai Yut) 65

Chop Sueys

Chicken and Pork Chop Suey (Gai Yuk
  Chee Yuk) 44
Chop Suey (Plain).................. 46
Duck Chop Suey.................... 42
Extra White Chop Suey............. 41
Gai Yuk Chee Yuk (Chicken and Pork
  Chop Suey)...................... 44
Gar Lu Chop Suey (with Chinese
  Dried Mushrooms)................ 43

Chow Mains

Chicken Chow Main................. 48
Lobster Chow Main................. 49
Meat Chow Main................... 47

Fish

Curry Shrimps...................... 25
Dried Shrimp Stew.................. 25
Fish Cakes (Yew)................... 23
Lobster Omelette................... 21
Pickled Fish, Cold................. 22

INDEX

	Page
Pineapple Fish	21
Shrimps, Curry	25
Shrimp Omelette	24
Sweet and Sour Fish (Ten Sune Gune)	20
Ten Sune Gune (Sweet and Sour Fish)	20
Yew (Fish Cakes)	23

FRIED RICE

Fried Rice with Chicken and Mushrooms	39
Fried Rice with Eggs and Herbs	52
Fried Rice with Herbs	52
Fried Rice with Tomato Sauce	52

GRAVY

Gravy	19
Gravy with Onions	19

MEATS

Beef, Fried, with Mushrooms	38
Beef Kidney with Chinese Mushrooms	37
Chinese Fried Pork with Onions	36
Fried Beef with Mushrooms	38
Fried Rice with Chicken and Mushrooms	39
Pepper Steak	37
Pork, Chinese Fried, with Onions	36
Pork with Green Peppers	36
Rice, Fried, with Chicken and Mushrooms	39

OMELETTES

Eggs, Chinese Scrambled	55
Foo Tay Dän (Chinese Ham and Eggs)	54
Foo Yung Dän (Chinese Omelette with Herbs)	54
Ham and Eggs, Chinese (Foo Tay Dän)	54

INDEX

	Page
Lobster Omelette........................	21
Mushroom Omelette....................	55
Scrambled Eggs, Chinese...............	55

POULTRY AND GAME

Boo Loo Gai (Pineapple Chicken)......	32
Chicken, Fried (Chinese Style)	27
Chicken, Fried, with Almonds or Walnuts (Hop Ho Gai Din).........	34
Chicken, Lychee......................	33
Chicken, Pineapple (Boo Loo Gai).....	32
Chicken, Sweet and Pungent..........	32
Chicken with Mushrooms.............	35
Duck, Steamed......................	30
Duck with Herbs....................	30
Fried Chicken (Chinese Style).........	27
Fried Chicken with Almonds or Walnuts (Hop Ho Gai Din).........	34
Fried Squab (Shu Bok Ap)............	27
Hop Ho Gai Din (Fried Chicken with Almonds or Walnuts)...............	34
Lychee Chicken......................	33
Pineapple Chicken (Boo Loo Gai)......	32
Roast Squab........................	29
Shu Bok Ap (Fried Squab)............	27
Squab, Fried (Shu Bok Ap)...........	27
Squab, Roast........................	29
Steamed Duck.......................	30
Sweet and Pungent Chicken..........	32

RULES FOR COOKING

Rice, to Boil........................	10
Tea...............................	11

SOUPS

Băk Toy T'ong (Chinese Soup of White Vegetables).................	17
Bird's-nest Soup (Gai Grun Yung Waa).............................	15

INDEX

Page

Gai Grun Yung Waa (Bird's-nest
 Soup)............................... 15
Mo Ku Gai T'ong (Spring Chicken
 Soup with Mushrooms)............. 14
Sea Weed Soup...................... 16
Soup Stock.......................... 13
Spring Chicken Soup with Mushrooms
 (Mo Ku Gai T'ong) 14
White Vegetables, Chinese Soup of
 (Băk Toy Gun).................... 17
Yat Ko Main........................ 12
Yea Foo Main....................... 12

VEGETABLES

Artichokes, Chinese (Char Quă)....... 61
Bamboo Shoots, Fried............... 60
Bean Sprouts, Fried................. 57
Boiled and Deviled Cucumbers....... 59
Cabbage, Fried..................... 57
Char Quă (Chinese Artichokes)....... 61
Cucumbers, Boiled and Deviled....... 59
Egg Plant.......................... 59
Endive............................. 58
Fried Bamboo Shoots................ 60
Fried Bean Sprouts................. 57
Fried Cabbage...................... 57
Fried Noodles...................... 63
Fried Peas, Chinese................ 62
Noodles, Fried..................... 63
Peas, Chinese, Fried............... 62
Pickled Yellow Turnips, Chinese...... 58
Seeds, Pumpkin or Yellow........... 63
Turnips, Chinese, Pickled, Yellow..... 58

PART II. JAPANESE RECIPES

FISH

Bass or Whale, Boiled (Mushi Kujira).. 75
Fish Balls, Japanese................. 78

INDEX

	Page
Fried Fish (Yaki Zakana)............	77
Lobster, Broiled (Onigara Yaki).......	77
Mushi Kujira (Boiled Whale or Bass)...	75
Onigara Yaki (Broiled Lobster).......	77
Tembani of Mackerel (Fish Delicacy)...	76
Whale or Bass, Boiled (Mushi Kujira)..	75
Yaki Zakana (Fried Fish)............	77

OMELETTES AND CUSTARDS

Cherry Custard (Sakura)............	90
Custard, Flower (Unohana Yaki)......	87
Eggs, Fried (Usu Tamago Yaki).......	89
Eggs, Peony (Tamago Bolan).........	91
Eggs, Scrambled (Japanese Style)......	90
Flower Custard (Unohana Yaki).......	87
Fried Eggs (Usu Tamago Yaki)........	89
Kinoko-Tamago-Yaki (Shrimp Omelette)	88
Peony Eggs (Tamago Bolan).........	91
Sakura (Cherry Custard)............	90
Scrambled Eggs (Japanese Style).......	90
Shrimp Omelette (Kinoko-Tamago-Yaki)	88
Tamago Tofu......................	89
Tamago Bolan (Peony Eggs)..........	91
Unohana Yaki (Flower Custard).......	87
Usu Tamago Yaki (Fried Eggs)........	89

POULTRY AND GAME

Baked Duck (Mushi Ahiru)...........	85
Chicken, Roast (Japanese Style).......	86
Duck, Baked (Mushi Ahiru)..........	85
Fried Squab......................	81
Hare, Sweet and Sour (Usagi Amai-Sui)	83
Hato Shiro (Stewed Pigeon)..........	81
Mushi Ahiru (Baked Duck)...........	85
Mushi Kiji (Roast Pheasant).........	82
Pheasant Roast (Mushi Kiji).........	82
Pigeon, Stewed (Hato Shiro).........	81
Pigeons or Quail, Broiled (Yaki Udzura)	79
Quail or Pigeons, Broiled (Yaki Udzura)	79

INDEX

Page

Roast Chicken (Japanese Style)........ 86
Roast Pheasant (Mushi Kiji).......... 82
Shika Shiro (Pot-roasted Venison) 80
Squab, Fried........................ 81
Stewed Pigeon (Hato Shiro).......... 81
Usagi Amai-Sui (Hare, Sweet and
  Sour)............................. 83
Venison, Pot-roasted (Shika Shiro) 80
Yaki Udzura (Broiled Quail or Pigeons). 79

SOUPS

Chicken Soup (Tori Shiru)........... 72
Fish Soup (Uwo Shiru) 73
Satsuma Soup....................... 71
Tori Shiru (Chicken Shiru)........... 72
Uwo Shiru (Fish Soup) 73

VEGETABLES AND RELISHES

Amai Tamana (Sweet and Sour
  Cabbage)......................... 96
Apple Jelly, Japanese Style (Ringo-
  Kan)............................. 102
Baked Bananas...................... 99
Bananas, Baked..................... 99
Bananas, Stuffed.................... 99
Cabbage and Pork (Mushi Tamana
  and Buta)........................ 94
Cabbage, Fried..................... 97
Cabbage, Satsuma Style (Satsuma
  Tamana)......................... 97
Cabbage, Sweet and Sour (Amai
  Tamana)......................... 96
Chicken Jelly (Tori-Kan)............ 100
Chicken Liver Paste................. 98
Eggplant, Fried (Nasubi Yaki) 96
Fried Cabbage...................... 97
Fried Eggplant (Nasubi Yaki)......... 96
Giblet Paste........................ 98
Karefish Nigore (Sole Jelly).......... 101

INDEX

Page

Kuwai-Kinton (Water Chestnut Cream) 93
Mushi Tamana and Buta (Cabbage
  and Pork)............................ 94
Nasubi Yaki (Fried Eggplant)......... 96
Paste, Chicken Liver................. 98
Paste, Giblet........................ 98
Plums, Sour and Sweet (Sumomo Sui
  and Amai)........................... 99
Pork and Cabbage (Mushi Tamana
  and Buta)........................... 94
Ringo-Kan (Apple Jelly, Japanese
  Style).............................. 102
Satsuma Tamana (Cabbage, Satsuma
  Style).............................. 97
Shiro Uri (Stewed Squash)............ 95
Sole Jelly (Karefish Nigore)......... 101
Squash, Stewed (Shiro Uri)........... 95
Stewed Squash (Shiro Uri)............ 95
Stuffed Bananas...................... 99
Sumomo Sui and Amai (Plums, Sour
  and Sweet).......................... 99
Tori-Kan (Chicken Jelly)............. 100
Water Chestnut Cream (Kuwai-
  Kinton)............................. 93

CAKES, CANDIES, SWEETMEATS

(Chinese and Japanese)

Bean Sprouts, How to Prepare........ 109
Beverages............................ 109
Chestnut Kintons (Cream Candy)...... 106
Cream Candy (Chestnut Kintons)...... 106
Dai-Kâm (Orange-Jelly Candy) 107
Katamochi............................ 104
Nut and Rice Candies................. 108
Orange-Jelly Candy (Dai-Kâm) 107
Owa Okashi........................... 106
Rice and Nut Candies................. 108

INDEX

	Page
San Char Go	105
Sweet Potato Candy	108
Yohan Candy	106
Yomoga Ga Shima	104
List of Groceries	111

CPSIA information can be obtained
at www.ICGtesting.com
Printed in the USA
BVHW080853191119
564175BV00008BA/689/P